THE WEIGHT OF THE BADGE AND THE HEART

By

A'Lexus Jones

Printed in the United States of America

First Edition

ISBN: 979-8-218-91776-0

CONTENTS

Prologue — The Weight 4

Chapter 1: Memories of the Child in Me 7

Chapter 2: Iraq 11

Chapter 3: Trouble in Paradise .17

Interlude Finding Myself 20

Chapter 4: Damn Gina 23

Chapter 5: I Stayed Too Long, So You Don't Have To 28

Chapter 6: Pressure Made Me 35

Chapter 7: Earned Not Given 42

Chapter 8: The Lessons Life Gave Me For Free 49

Chapter 9: He Met Me While I Was Becoming 58

Chapter 10: When Strength Learned My Name 63

Acknowledgements 66

Disclaimer 70

PROLOGUE — THE WEIGHT

I never understood the weight of a badge until the day I put one on. People think it's the metal that's heavy, the authority, the responsibility. But the real weight comes from everything you carry underneath it — the childhood you survived, the people who doubted you, the ones who loved you, the ones who tried to break you, and the ones you're still trying to forgive.

Before I ever stepped into a uniform, I was just Allie — the fifth out of six kids in a house that was always loud, always moving, always full of something. Mama and Daddy were very young when they got married and started having kids. By the time I came along, they were already tired, already fighting battles I didn't understand until much later.

Daddy was my best friend. Still is. He's a Sergeant, the kind of man who leads with his chest and his heart at the same time. One of my brothers wears the badge too. In my family, law enforcement isn't just a job — it's a legacy, a language, a shadow you grow up under whether you want to or not. I didn't know if I wanted to follow that path, but I knew I wanted to make Daddy proud. I always did.

Mama… that's a different story. She loved me, but her love came with conditions, with expectations, with wounds she never healed from. She blamed me for things that were never mine to carry. She once told me I could've stopped the divorce, like I had the power to fix a marriage that broke long before I was old enough to understand what marriage even meant. She held my past over my head, tried to make me feel like I owed her for decisions she made when I was fourteen and fifteen. But Daddy already knew the truth. I told him myself. I wasn't built to carry secrets that heavy.

And then there was Dro. Ten years of my life tied up in a man who started out as everything I thought I needed — funny, sweet, adventurous, the kind of guy who made me feel alive when I didn't even know I was numb. I met him when my oldest daughter "Krystal" was two, and for a while, he felt like home. But homes can turn into prisons. Love can turn into fear. And the man who once made me laugh became the man who tried to dim every part of me that shined. Daddy never approved. Mama liked him. That should've told me everything.

When I started the academy, Dro gave me nothing. Not support, not encouragement, not even the bare minimum. Morris stepped in. He always did. He became the uncle my daughters, "Krystal and Kellie" adored, the brother who held me up when I didn't think I could keep going. And somewhere in the middle of all that chaos, all that pain, all that rebuilding, I met Edward. The man who would later become my peace, my partner, my fiancé. But that part of the story comes later.

This book isn't about perfection. It's about truth. My truth.

The truth of a girl who grew up in the middle of a storm.

The truth of a woman who learned to carry a badge and a broken heart at the same time.

The truth of a mother who fought like hell to give her daughters a life she never had.

The truth of a daughter who loved her father fiercely and struggled to love her mother without losing herself.

The truth of someone who survived things she never talked about, things she never thought she'd write down.

This is my story — the weight I carried, the heart I protected, and the badge I earned.

And I'm finally ready to tell it.

CHAPTER 1

"MEMORIES OF THE CHILD IN ME"

Our house was always alive — loud, warm, crowded, and overflowing with people. Six kids under one roof meant there was always something happening. Somebody laughing, somebody arguing, somebody getting into something they shouldn't, somebody running through the house like they didn't have good sense. I was the fifth child, right in the middle of it all, soaking up the noise and the love like air.

We were close. All of us. Tight-knit in a way that felt normal back then, but looking back, it was rare. We had family nights all the time — the kind where everybody piled into the living room, talking over each other, cracking jokes, watching movies, or playing games. And every weekend, without fail, we broke bread with other families or friends. It didn't matter whose house it was — ours, theirs, somebody's cousin's — we were there. Food, laughter, kids running around, grown folks talking loud, music playing in the background. That was our life. That was our rhythm.

From as early as I can remember all the way up until my early 10th-grade year, we were like our own version of the Brady Bunch — just with more personality, more attitude, and a whole lot more noise. Me and my siblings were always together. We played outside until the streetlights came on, rode bikes, made up games, fought, made up again, and did it all over the next day. We were each other's first friends, first enemies, first protectors. There was a closeness between us that felt unbreakable.

Mama was young, married at sixteen and had her first child at eighteen. But she was present, She was involved. That didn't stop her from being a mother, wife, or friend. She was fun when she wanted to be, strict when she needed to be, and always in the mix of whatever we had going on. She cooked, she laughed, she fussed, she danced, she talked mess — she was Mama. And back then, me and her were close. I didn't feel distance or tension or anything heavy between us. That came later. Before Iraq, she was just my mother, the only woman I was close to, and I loved being around her.

Daddy was the anchor of our house. Strong, steady, dependable. He worked hard, came home tired, but still made time for us — especially me. I don't know if it was because I was the second to youngest or because he saw something in me that reminded him of himself, but Daddy and I had a bond that didn't need many words. He was my best friend long before I understood what that meant.

Even though Mama and Daddy had their moments — and they did — there was still a sense of unity in our home. A sense of "we." A sense that no matter what happened, we were a family first. We had routines, traditions, and a closeness that wrapped around us like a blanket.

Before Iraq, I didn't know what it felt like to miss Daddy.

I didn't know what it felt like to worry every day.

I didn't know what it felt like to watch Mama struggle without him.

I didn't know what it felt like to grow up faster than I wanted to.

Before Iraq, I was still just a kid.

A kid in a big, loud, loving family.

A kid with a Daddy who came home every night.

A kid who thought things would always stay the same.

I didn't know that everything was about to change.

I didn't know that the man who held our house together would soon be half a world away.

I didn't know that Mama would have to carry the weight of the world on her own.

I didn't know that I would have to become stronger than I ever planned to be.

All I knew was the life we had before Daddy left — warm, tight-knit, full of love and noise and people.

A life I didn't realize I cherished until the day it disappeared.

———————— ✦◆✦ ————————

Isaiah 43:2

"When you pass through the waters, I will be with you; And through the rivers, they will not overwhelm you. When you walk through fire, you will not be scorched, Nor will the flame burn you."

CHAPTER 2

"IRAQ"

When Daddy left for Iraq, it felt like someone had pulled the center out of our home. We still had family nights, still had people over, still had laughter — but underneath it all, something felt off. I didn't have the words for it then, but I felt it. A shift. A looseness. Like the house wasn't held together the same way anymore.

My oldest brother's best friend Maurice and his family came over often. They had always been around, part of our circle, part of the noise and comfort of our weekends. But once he learned Daddy was gone, something in his behavior changed. I started noticing him standing in my doorway, watching me. At first, I didn't know what to make of it. I was young, still trusting, still believing people were who they pretended to be.

The day he motioned for me to come toward him, I didn't think anything bad would happen. I didn't know I needed to be afraid. But the moment he crossed a line, something inside me froze. My mind went blank except for one thought; This doesn't feel right. He began to tug on my clothes attempting to remove them, then he forced himself on top of me holding me down groping my intimate body parts and trying to kiss me, I kept turning my head back & forth trying to avoid his lips from touching mine. I felt confused, scared, and small. I didn't understand why he was doing it or why I felt so wrong inside. I just knew I needed to get away. When I finally broke free and ran outside to play with my siblings, I pretended nothing happened because pretending felt safer than trying to understand something I didn't have the language for.

The next week, when his family came over again, I felt dread instead of excitement. My stomach twisted the moment I heard their voices. And when he walked straight to my room without hesitation, I knew exactly why. He didn't knock. He didn't ask. He just came in. I felt trapped, powerless, like my voice didn't belong to me. I felt like I was living out a bad case of Deja Vu, I turned my head away, trying to escape in the only way I could. When he finally stopped touching me, I felt hollow — like something inside me had spilled out. One thing I was and still am grateful for is that I spoke up, and I believe that is what stopped him from going any further than just physical touch.

I thought Mama would protect me. I thought telling her would make it stop. I thought she would hold me, believe me, shield me. Instead, she told me to be quiet. Then she told other people what I had shared with her in confidence. Suddenly, I was surrounded by whispers, accusations, and siblings — mine and his — calling me a liar. I cried because I knew the one person who would have believed me without hesitation was thousands of miles away. Daddy. I didn't know that the moment he left, my protection would leave with him.

But life didn't pause for my pain. School kept going. People kept coming over. And somewhere in the middle of all that confusion, I met a boy from Pontiac who had just moved to the city. He was a little older, and he made me feel seen at a time when I felt invisible. He made me feel chosen, wanted, understood — things I didn't realize I was craving until he gave them to me. We liked each other. We started dating. And I kept him a secret because secrets had become normal to me. I didn't trust anyone with the truth anymore.

Around this time, Daddy came home from Iraq. Everyone was excited. The house felt alive again. But inside, I felt split in two. Part of me wanted to run to him, tell him everything, let him fix what had been broken. But another part of me felt ashamed, scared he'd look at me differently, scared he'd be disappointed. So I kept quiet. I smiled. I hugged him. And I hid everything I was going through.

No one knew about the boy from school. No one knew what had happened with Maurice. No one knew how heavy my heart felt. I carried it all alone.

Months passed, and I noticed changes in my body and a little weight gain, but I didn't understand what was happening. I didn't have the language, the guidance, or the space to ask questions. I just kept going, pretending everything was normal.

Then one night, everything changed again.

I woke up in the middle of the night with a pain so sharp it bent me over. I tried to walk, each step worse than the last. I thought maybe I was sick, maybe I needed to use the bathroom. But when I turned on the light, I saw something that terrified me, BLOOD! and lots of it! I didn't understand what was happening — only that something was very wrong.

I tried to steady myself, tried to breathe through the pain, tried to make sense of what my body was doing. And then, in a moment that felt unreal, I realized I was losing something, I was miscarrying a baby that I didn't even know I was carrying in the first place. I heard a thud sound drop into the toilet, I stood up slowly and looked, and that's when I saw the small bloody fetus, not fully developed lying in the toilet.

Then I heard a noise in the hallway and panicked, thinking Mama or Daddy had woken up. But it was Morris. My brother. The one who always seemed to show up when I needed someone most. He stood in the doorway with his hand over his mouth, shocked! trying to understand what he was seeing. Then he asked if I was okay — over and over — and helped me clean myself up, helped me steady my breathing, helped me feel less alone.

Hours passed. The sun came up. And when it was time for school, I got dressed and walked out the door like nothing had happened. Because in that moment of my life, pretending felt safer than telling the truth.

I didn't know it then, but Iraq wasn't just the place Daddy went.

It was the moment everything in my world shifted.

The moment childhood ended.

The moment I learned what it felt like to be unprotected.

The moment I realized I would have to survive things on my own.

Years passed after Daddy came home from Iraq the first time. Life felt like it was trying to settle back into something familiar, but nothing ever went back to the way it was before he left. I was older now, carrying secrets I didn't have the courage to speak out loud, and trying to make sense of the pieces of myself I had lost along the way.

Just when I thought things were finally stabilizing, Daddy told us he had to leave again. Back to Iraq. Back to the place that had already taken so much from him — and from us. I remember feeling numb. Not shocked. Not angry. Just… tired. Tired of goodbyes. Tired of pretending I was okay. Tired of trying to be strong when I still felt like a child inside.

While Daddy was gone again, I was still dealing with the boy from Pontiac — the one I thought I loved. The one who made me feel seen when I felt invisible. I kept sneaking him in and out of the house, thinking I was grown, thinking I was in control, thinking what we had was love. But it wasn't love. It was lust, infatuation, and the kind of attention I mistook for affection because I didn't know any better. Once I realized he never cared about me, he only wanted me for my body that's when I made up my mind and ended things with him. Regardless of all his begging and pleading, I was done.

When I found out I was pregnant again, my heart dropped. I didn't cry. I didn't panic. I just felt… heavy. Like life kept handing me things I wasn't ready for. I told Mama I wanted an abortion, and she didn't hesitate. She took me, paid the $500, and told me we would never tell Daddy. She said we would take it to the grave. And I believed her. I trusted her. I thought she was protecting me.

A few months passed, and Daddy finally came home for good. I wanted to be happy. I wanted to run to him like I used to. But I felt distant from myself, and that distance made me feel distant from him too. I had changed. Life had changed. And I didn't know how to bridge the gap.

✦◆✦

Romans 8:28

*"And we know that in all things God works for
the good of those who love him, who have been
called according to his purpose."*

CHAPTER 3

"TROUBLE IN PARADISE"

Fast forward to Daddy's first day back on the streets of Flint as an officer — the day everything shifted again. He got injured on duty during an altercation. Broke numerous bones in his leg. Needed surgery. Rods and Screws. This was a long recovery for daddy. Daddy wasn't the type to sit still, and not being able to provide for the family the way he always did, was tearing him up inside. I could see the frustration in his eyes, the stress in his shoulders, the weight he carried even when he tried to hide it.

Mama changed too. She helped him, but her energy was different. Cold. Irritated. Like he was a burden instead of her husband. I didn't understand it. I didn't recognize her. The same woman who used to fuss and laugh and dance around the house now seemed annoyed by Daddy's very presence.

One day, they got into an argument. I don't remember what it was about — I just remember the sound of Mama's voice, sharp and angry, and the way she stormed out of the house afterward. I watched her walk outside, phone in hand, and then I heard her call Gina. I heard her venting, complaining, telling her things that felt too personal to share with another woman.

I remember asking Mama, "Why is you calling her?"

Not out of disrespect, but confusion.

Why bring another woman into your marriage?

Why put our family business in someone else's hands?

Mama brushed me off, but something in my spirit felt unsettled.

Slowly, I started to see their marriage unravel. Daddy began opening up about things he had heard — rumors of infidelity, whispers from an unknown source who had been feeding him information ever since he had been back home from Iraq. He told me how hard it was being over there, how lonely and how mentally draining it was. How he thought of Mama back home. Daddy said while experiencing all of this he would always Skype to talk to us and when he would call, all Mama would say was, "Why you keep calling me?", "What you want?", "The kids ain't here", all while knowing his family was the only thing that kept him going some days. And now, he didn't know what to believe.

Everything felt confusing.

Everything felt heavy.

Everything felt wrong.

But at that time, I still thought Gina was just Mama and Daddy's friend. Someone who had been around for years. Someone Mama trusted. Someone Daddy respected. I didn't see the cracks yet. I didn't see the truth forming in the shadows.

But lies don't stay hidden forever.

Secrets don't stay buried.

And the truth — the real truth — was getting ready to reveal itself in ways none of us were prepared for.

This was the beginning of the unraveling.

The beginning of the betrayal.

The beginning of the forgiveness I'm still trying to find.

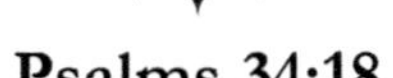

Psalms 34:18
"The Lord is close to the brokenhearted and saves those who are crushed in spirit."

INTERLUDE "FINDING MYSELF"

Fast forward to my early college years, life felt like it was moving faster than I could keep up with. I was still trying to figure out who I was, still carrying pieces of my past that I hadn't healed from, still trying to make sense of the girl I used to be and the woman I was becoming.

Somewhere in the middle of all that confusion, I found myself pregnant again. This time, when I told Mama, she didn't hesitate. She didn't ask questions or get upset. She just said, "You keeping this one." And I did. That's how my baby girl Krystal came into my life — the first person who ever made me feel like I had a purpose bigger than my pain. She was born into my arms and healed parts of me she'll never see.

God sent me my child when I needed saving.

Daddy was always against the idea of me going into law enforcement. He knew the dangers, the stress, the toll it took on a person. He had lived it. But he also knew my heart. He knew I wanted to walk in his footsteps, not because I wanted to be like him, but because I wanted to provide for my kids the way he provided for us. Law enforcement was the only example of stability I had ever seen. It was the only blueprint I knew.

Around this time, I met Dro — Kellie's dad. I was working at Checkers when I met him, and he was nothing like the boys I grew up around. He was funny, down-to-earth, adventurous, and familiar with a world Daddy always kept us sheltered from. After I left Checkers for a better opportunity at Hurley Hospital, me and Dro got even closer. I spent a lot of time with him on the north side of Flint — in the hood, at clubs, at house parties, in places Daddy would've had a fit about. But back then, it felt exciting. It felt freeing. It felt like I was finally seeing a world I had only heard stories about.

When me and Dro started dating, I kept him a secret from Daddy for six months. Not because I was ashamed, but because I already knew Daddy wouldn't approve. Dro was the type of guy Daddy warned us about — the popular one, the street-familiar one, the one who could charm a room but didn't have much direction. I didn't want to hear Daddy's judgment. I didn't want to be told I was making a mistake. I wanted to figure it out on my own.

A year later, me and Dro welcomed our baby girl Kellie into the world. She was beautiful, loud, full of personality — a perfect mix of both of us. We moved in together, trying to build a family, trying to make it work, trying to create something stable out of two unstable people.

But reality hit fast.

I found myself juggling motherhood with two little girls, working long hours, trying to keep the house together, trying to be everything for everybody. Meanwhile, Dro stayed out late — sometimes all night — clubbing, drinking, living like he didn't have responsibilities waiting for him at home. I would be up with the girls, exhausted, frustrated, wondering how I ended up carrying everything on my own again.

I didn't realize it then, but I was losing myself.

Not all at once — slowly. Quietly.

Piece by piece.

This was the beginning of me learning who I was outside of my family, outside of my relationships, outside of the expectations people placed on me. It was messy. It was painful. But it was the start of me finding myself — even if I didn't know it yet.

CHAPTER 4

"DAMN GINA"

I never expected Mama to be the one to break my heart first.

When she told me Daddy was cheating, she said it like she wanted a reaction out of me — like she wanted me to hurt with her, or for her, or maybe even because of her. I remember the way her voice sounded, sharp and shaky at the same time. I remember the way my stomach dropped. I remember feeling sad, upset, confused — like the ground under me had cracked open.

I called Daddy immediately. I didn't know what else to do. I needed answers. I needed the truth. I needed to hear his voice.

When he picked up, I could hear the heaviness in his breathing before he even spoke.

"Even though I don't want to tell you this," he said, "I'd never lie to you."

And that's when he told me everything — the truth Mama left out.

The truth she twisted.

The truth she weaponized.

Daddy told me about the choice they made together, the decision to invite another person into their marriage. Something they both agreed to. Something Mama had allowed. Something Mama had participated in. Something Mama had introduced into their home long before it became a secret.

Hearing that made my chest tighten.

Not because of what they did — but because Mama lied to me about it.

Because she made Daddy the villain in a story she helped write.

After that, their marriage started falling apart fast. It was like watching a slow leak turn into a flood. Arguments. Distance. Silence. Tension that filled the house like smoke.

One day, I was getting my hair braided when everything exploded.

Mama was at HomeGoods and saw Daddy at a nearby gas station with Gina — the same Gina who had been around our family for years. The same Gina Mama called her friend. The same Gina who worked in Mama's salon. The same Gina Mama had invited into their marriage.

But in that moment, Mama acted like she had no part in any of it.

She called me, her voice shaking with anger, and said,

"Your dad is cheating with that bitch. Go look at her Instagram."

I didn't want to look. I didn't want to see anything that would make my heart hurt more. But I did. And there they were — pictures of Daddy's hands, the interior of his white Corvette, little hints that confirmed what Mama wanted me to believe.

Except the truth was more complicated than the story she was telling.

Mama wasn't just hurt — she was trying to turn me against Daddy.

Trying to make me pick a side.

Trying to make me carry her pain.

But Daddy had never lied to me.

Not once.

Not ever.

Mama, on the other hand…

She started saying things to me that cut deeper than anything I had ever heard from her.

She talked to me like I was a stranger off the street.

Like I was the enemy.

Like I was the reason her world was falling apart.

And then she did something I never saw coming — she stopped speaking to my kids.

My babies.

Her granddaughters.

The same little girls who used to run to her with open arms.

Her world was ending, and instead of holding on to the people who loved her, she kept breaking mine.

I didn't know how to process any of it.

I didn't know how to forgive her.

I didn't know how to understand a mother who could turn her pain into a weapon.

That was the moment I realized Gina wasn't just a friend.

She was the truth Mama didn't want to face.

She was the secret Mama tried to twist into a lie.

She was the woman Daddy told me about — honestly, painfully, reluctantly.

And she was the beginning of the fracture that would change our family forever.

All I knew was that the woman who raised me wasn't the same woman standing in front of me now.

And the girl who used to run to Mama for comfort was gone too.

This was the beginning of a wound I'm still trying to heal.

The beginning of a truth I'm still trying to accept.

— ✦◆✦ —

James 1:2-4

"Consider it pure joy, my brothers and sisters, whenever you face trials of many kinds, because you know that the testing of your faith produces perseverance. Let perseverance finish its work so that you may be mature and complete, not lacking anything."

CHAPTER 5

"I STAYED TOO LONG, SO YOU DON'T HAVE TO"

By 2017, I was tired of feeling stuck. Tired of feeling like life was happening to me instead of through me. So I made the decision to apply at the Genesee County Sheriff's Office. Deep down, I wanted to be a police officer — a real one, like Daddy. But Daddy insisted I stay away from the streets. He told me being a turnkey, a deputy inside the jail, was safer. "More like me," he said. And because I loved him, because I trusted him, because I still wanted to make him proud, I listened.

I stayed there for four and a half years.

Four and a half years of feeling like I was close to my dream but not quite living it.

Four and a half years of convincing myself I was doing the right thing.

Four and a half years of illusions.

Working inside the jail was its own world. Loud. Violent. Heavy. I remember the day I got assigned to an all-male floor — me, the only woman on the unit. I walked in with my head high, but inside, I felt the weight of every eye on me.

And then I saw him.

Maurice.

My brother's old best friend.

The same boy who stole pieces of my childhood.

The same boy who taught me what fear felt like before I even understood the word.

He walked up to my desk like we were old friends and said, "I'm sorry."

Then he asked how I'd been.

In that moment, the little girl in me froze.

I felt the humiliation.

The confusion.

The anger.

The shame I carried alone for years.

All of it rushed back like it had been waiting for him to show his face again.

But the woman in me — the one who had survived, the one who had grown, the one who refused to break — she answered for me.

"I been well," I said, even though my voice felt like it belonged to someone else.

After he walked away, I pulled up his charges in the system.

CSC — Criminal Sexual Conduct. Twice.

I wasn't shocked.

Not even a little.

Some people spend their whole lives running from the truth, but karma always knows where to find them. And I always knew, karma would come clean his plate.

During those years, I gained weight — the heaviest I had ever been.

252 pounds.

I didn't recognize myself.

I didn't feel like myself.

But I kept pushing, kept trying, kept chasing the dream Daddy didn't want for me.

I took the MCOLES physical agility test fifteen times.

Fifteen.

And I failed it every single time.

Each failure felt like a punch to the chest.

Each failure made me question my worth.

Each failure made me wonder if Daddy had been right all along.

But I refused to quit.

One day, after failing again, I was getting ready to go train with Daddy — because no matter how many times I fell, he was always there to help me get back up. Dro was cutting somebody's hair in the living room when he stopped me and said,

"That job ain't for you."

Then, with a smirk,

"You leave with yo daddy so much you might as well be fucking him."

I felt sick.

Disgusted.

Hurt in a way I didn't have words for.

"How can you say something like that," I asked him, "when you see I'm trying to win?"

But Dro didn't care about my dreams.

He didn't care about my goals.

He didn't care about anything that didn't revolve around him.

What Dro didn't understand was that Daddy hated seeing me settle for less. He hated watching me suffer in a relationship with a man who never deserved me. Daddy set the bar high for me and my siblings — not with money, but with love, protection, and consistency. He showed us what a real man looked like, how a real man treats his family, how a real man shows up. And deep down, I knew Dro wasn't living up to any of that.

What started out as rebellion — choosing someone Daddy would never approve of — started to feel more like embarrassment. I was outgrowing the version of myself that tolerated bare minimum love. I knew I had to do better, not just for Daddy, not just for my girls, but for the woman I was becoming."

I was drained — taking care of the house, the kids, paying all the bills, working full-time — while Dro stayed out partying, drinking, living like he didn't have a family at home. My brother Morris was the one who showed up for me. Morris was the one who helped with the girls. Morris was the one who made sure I wasn't drowning alone.

Dro couldn't even remember to pick me up from work most mornings after a 12 hour shift.

He'd be drunk, out somewhere, forgetting about me.

I'd have to catch rides home with coworkers, embarrassed and exhausted.

Then one night, while I was at work at the Sheriff's Office, I got a call that Dro had been shot in the head — on Facebook Live. My heart dropped, not because I still loved him the same, but because he was the father of my child. Because no matter how much he hurt me, I didn't want him dead.

Life didn't slow down, though.

Not for him.

Not for me.

Months went by, Dro healed. But things weren't getting any easier for me. One day I left work mad, depressed, overwhelmed, and I got into a bad car accident. I don't know how Daddy got to me so fast — it felt like he appeared out of thin air. When EMS arrived, Daddy was already trying to put me in his car to rush me to the hospital himself. He didn't trust them. He didn't trust anyone with me. But they convinced him to let them take me.

Mama even showed up at the hospital.

But Dro?

The man who claimed to love me?

The man who lived in my house?

The man I had a child with?

He didn't show up.
Not then.

Not even when it mattered.

Six months later, I got into the Flint Police Academy.

Dro knew I was training.

He knew I was fighting for my dream.

He knew I was pushing myself harder than I ever had before.

But what he didn't know was that I wasn't just training my body.

I was training my mind.

Training my heart.

Training my spirit.

I was preparing to leave a relationship that no longer served me.

A relationship that drained me.

A relationship that dimmed me.

A relationship that taught me the difference between love and illusion.

And this time, I told myself I wasn't going to fail.

Proverbs 3:5-6

"Trust in the Lord with all your heart and lean not on your own understanding; in all your ways submit to him, and he will make your paths straight."

CHAPTER 6

"PRESSURE MADE ME"

I started the Flint Police Academy in 2021. Four months. That's what they told us. Four months of training, discipline, studying, and pushing your body and mind past limits you didn't even know existed. I walked in nervous but hopeful, thinking this was finally my moment. My chance. My time.

But the moment I stepped through those doors, I realized I had walked into another battlefield.

I was shocked to see that one of my instructors was someone I already knew — PO Long. We had worked together at the Sheriff's Office. I thought that meant familiarity. Maybe even support. But instead, it felt like I had gained another enemy. She failed me on tests, questioned everything I did, and made my academy days harder than they needed to be. Every time I looked up, she was there — watching, waiting, almost hoping I'd fall apart.

And the truth was… I didn't understand anything they were teaching. The objectives felt like a foreign language. Everyone else seemed to catch on faster, move faster, think faster. I felt like I was drowning in a room full of people who were breathing just fine.

Sgt. Collins noticed. One day he pulled me aside and said,

"Some people are intimidated by your energy."

I didn't know whether to take that as a compliment or a warning.

All I knew was that I was failing — academically, mentally, emotionally.

Every day I walked into class feeling depressed, like maybe this wasn't my time.

Like maybe I wasn't meant for this.

And right in the middle of all that pressure, Mama called me on my very first day of the academy. Not to check on me. Not to encourage me. Not to ask how I was holding up.

She called to talk about her marriage.

To accuse me — again — of knowing she was cheating on Daddy.

To drag me into something that had nothing to do with me.

I told her, "I had a rough day. I'm not up to talk about this. Your marriage has nothing to do with me. I'm your daughter, not your friend."

Her response?

"Don't forget what I did for you."

She said it like a threat.

Like she was holding my abortion over my head.

Like she owned my silence.

Like she owned me.

And something in me snapped.

Not in anger — in clarity.

I hung up with Mama and immediately called Daddy.

I was tired.

Tired of carrying secrets.

Tired of being manipulated.

Tired of being treated like a child when I was a grown woman with kids of my own.

When Daddy answered, I told him everything.

The abortion.

The truth Mama thought she could use to control me.

The truth she assumed I'd never say out loud.

I told him because I needed to be free.

I told him because I was done letting Mama hold anything over my head.

I told him because I trusted him more than anyone in the world.

Daddy didn't yell.

He didn't judge me.

He didn't make me feel ashamed.

He just listened — the way he always did — and told me he loved me.

That moment changed something in me.

It was the first time I realized I didn't owe Mama my silence.

I didn't owe her my secrets.

I didn't owe her my guilt.

I owed myself peace.

Daddy, on the other hand, wanted me to write a letter for the courts during their divorce. He wanted me to speak on what I knew. But all I could write about was the heartbreak of losing my closeness with Mama. That was the only truth I had. The only thing I could speak on without betraying myself.

And then, after all the mental and physical stress, after all the studying, after all the tears, after all the nights I stayed up trying to understand material that never clicked…

I failed the Flint Police Academy.

Flint told me they wouldn't sponsor me again.

Just like that — my dream was gone.

And the thought of walking back into the Sheriff's Office felt humiliating.

Like I'd be walking back into failure with my head down.

But I kept pushing.

I kept striving.

I kept fighting for something I couldn't let go of.

When I failed, Lt. Love — God rest his soul — pulled me aside. He looked me in my eyes and said,

"You're going to be great. This doesn't stop here. A delay is never a deny."

Then he said the words I still hear in my head today:

"If you have integrity, nothing else matters. If you don't have integrity, nothing else matters."

I think about his words often.

Especially on the days I feel like giving up.

But then came the final blow — I failed my last chance at the written exam.

And just like that, I lost everything.

My job.

My stability.

My confidence.

My sense of direction.

I didn't know how I was going to maintain my house.

How I was going to take care of my kids.

How I was going to keep going when everything felt like it was falling apart.

Daddy stepped in.

Like he always did.

He paid all my bills when I couldn't.

He let me cry for three days straight.

He didn't rush me.

He didn't judge me.

He didn't tell me to toughen up.

He just let me be human.

But on day four, he called me and said,

"Get up. Let's go get it again."

And just like that, we were back to training.

Back to fighting.

Back to chasing the dream that refused to let me go.

Pressure didn't break me.

Galatians 6:9

"Let us not become weary in doing good, for at the proper time we will reap a harvest if we do not give up."

CHAPTER 7

"EARNED NOT GIVEN"

After losing everything, I spent a week to myself. No noise. No distractions. No pretending. Just me, my thoughts, and a Bible I didn't fully understand. I would open it and stare at the pages, hoping something would jump out at me. I would pray even though I didn't know what to say. Half the time, all I could manage was, "God… help me." And somehow, that felt like enough.

Dro would come in the room trying to play "man of the house," saying things like, "I got us, ima be the head of the house, I'm paying all the bills."

Which was wild, because he never kept a job. He was cutting hair here and there at the house, barely making enough to buy himself a bottle, let alone support a family.

So besides training with Daddy, I stayed in my room detoxing my mind. Resetting. Rebuilding. I felt like God wanted His one-on-one time with me — no interruptions, no noise, no chaos. Just me and Him.

Then it hit me — God was writing a test for me that no piece of paper could measure. My journey wasn't supposed to look like anyone else's. My brother followed in Daddy's footsteps and passed everything with ease, becoming an amazing officer. And I kept wondering why my path felt so different... why every step felt like a battle.

But in that moment, I realized something important:

My story required a different kind of strength.

My testimony needed a different kind of fight.

So I toughened up. I stopped comparing my journey to anyone else's and accepted that what God was building in me required pressure, patience, and perseverance.

One day, I went to the gym with Daddy and told him I applied for Detroit Police Department. It had only been a week since I lost everything, but something in me refused to stay down. Within a week of applying, I got a call back — but I still had to retake my physical agility test to be considered for the academy.

Daddy drove me to the test, and I failed my police run by 30 seconds.

Thirty seconds.

Thirty seconds between me and the life I wanted.

But I was determined to be in the February 2022 academy class. So when I walked into the Detroit Police Academy to retest, I came ready. I saw women dressed like they were going to a club — tight clothes, long weave, long nails, lashes touching their eyebrows. But I wasn't there for a fashion show. I had on a big T-shirt, gym shorts, and two braids to the back like I was one of the guys. I came to work like my life depended on it.

When the test started, I ran as hard as I could — just like Daddy trained me. I thought I did my best. But when they told me I failed again, I felt the defeat hit me like a punch to the chest.

As I was walking out, Sgt. Greene — one of the strongest female sergeants there — stopped me. She looked me dead in my eyes and said,

"You better hold it together. Keep your head up. You ain't quitting. I'll see you next week."

She must've seen the heartbreak all over my face.

I walked to the car, and Daddy asked, "Did you get it?"

I said, "No… but I will."

And I meant it.

A few minutes later, the recruiting officer called me.

"You missed it by 30 seconds. What happened?"

"I'm going back Saturday to retest," I told him. "I know what I need to do."

He said, "Okay, this is your final chance. If you don't make it this time, I can't push you through this academy."

When I hung up, Daddy didn't waste a second.

"Come on," he said. "We got more work to do."

Daddy was still recovering from that major injury he had awhile back — the one that left him with rods and screws in his leg — but regardless of his own pain, he still got in the field with me and trained. He pushed through every ache, every limitation, just to make sure I didn't give up on myself.

I was tired — physically, mentally, emotionally.

But Daddy pushed me like only he could.

While I ran, he yelled things like,

"If you ain't passed out or dead, you ain't tired enough — keep running! "You better get comfortable with being uncomfortable", or

"Nothing comes to a sleeper but a dream — keep running!"

I hated it in the moment, but I needed it.

I needed someone to believe in me louder than the doubt in my own head.

The final week of testing came, and my stomach felt like it was in my ass. I was scared, nervous, anxious — but ready.

This time, Daddy came inside the academy with me instead of waiting in the car. He walked in smiling, coffee in hand, saying,

"Come on, let's go get this win. I'm excited!"

Seeing the other people there made me even more nervous. My stomach was doing the Watusi, but I told myself not to overthink it. Just take my time. One test at a time.

I passed the first test.

Then the second.

Then the third.

Then came the fourth — the agility run.

The one that had been beating me.

The one standing between me and my future.

I said, "Set."

The test proctor said, "Go."

And I took off.

Daddy was at the end of the hall waiting for me — waiting for a win.

The proctor counted out laps 5… 10… 13…

My heart was beating out of my chest.

My legs were burning.

My lungs felt like they were on fire.

But all I could hear was Daddy's voice in my head:

"Go get yo job."

And I did.

When I finished, the proctor said, "Passed."

He showed me my score — I beat it by 30 seconds.

The same 30 seconds that defeated me last time were the 30 seconds I conquered today.

I walked into the corner and cried.

Not quiet tears — the kind that come from your soul.

People looked at me crazy, but they didn't know this was personal.

They didn't know what I had survived to get here.

After I pulled myself together, I walked down the hallway toward Daddy. Tears still in my eyes. He was still holding his coffee.

"Did you get it? Did you pass?"

"Yes," I said.

We hugged each other so tightly.

We cried.

Because we trained for this.

We fought for this.

We earned this.

Thirty minutes later, the recruiting officer called.

He was amazed.

He asked how I shaved off 30 seconds in one week — said he'd never seen that before.

Then he gave me my drug screening date, my psychological exam, and my orientation date to sign my hiring papers for Detroit Police Department.

I didn't just get in.

I earned it.

Every tear.

Every failure.

Every mile.

Every prayer.

Every second.

Earned.

Not given.

Philippians 4:13
"I can do all this through Christ who gives me strength."

CHAPTER 8

"THE LESSONS LIFE GAVE ME FOR FREE"

The first day of the Detroit Police Academy felt like stepping into a world I had only imagined from the outside. Twenty-seven people stood in that room — twenty-seven strangers with different stories, different reasons for being there, different levels of confidence. I didn't know a soul. Detroit was new to me. The people were new. The environment was new. But my purpose wasn't.

It was an hour drive there and an hour drive back every single day.

Two hours of thinking.

Two hours of praying.

Two hours of reminding myself why I was doing this.

Some people walked in treating the academy like it was just another job. But I wasn't there for a paycheck. I was there to rewrite my life. I was there because my daughters needed a mother who didn't quit. I was there because Daddy believed in me when I didn't believe in myself. I was there because I refused to let failure be the last chapter of my story.

Two minutes after we lined up, the instructors stormed in yelling and cussing like they were trying to break the walls off the building. I had no idea it was a quasi-military academy. I knew it would be strict, but I didn't know they were coming on tip like that. They reminded us daily that they were not our friends.

I remember thinking, "Wtf did I get myself into?"

Out of twenty-seven students, only me and one other girl were women.

The yelling didn't bother me — life had already yelled at me louder than any instructor ever could — but the intensity was something else.

When we got outside, one of the male instructors got right in my face and yelled,

"YOU READY FOR THIS SHIT?!"

I said, "Sir yes sir!"

He was breaking people down left and right. Some of them didn't know how to manage. But not me. I had already been broken before — by life, by love, by betrayal, by disappointment. This wasn't new. This wasn't scary. This was familiar.

Everybody got a piece of it while we stood in line holding our belongings over our heads, jogging in place. They didn't care if you had books or bricks in your bag.

I was the only one who had just come out of another academy, so I was prepared. This was all new to the others. I just stood face-forward and made sure not to look the instructors in the eyes. Being surrounded by all men was intimidating, but I kept going.

After the verbal and mental torment, they told us to run. They made us dress in white button-ups, ties, black dress pants, and shiny black shoes. Anytime we addressed them, it had to be "sir yes sir" or "ma'am no ma'am." They were building structure and discipline — but they were also testing who would fold.

One guy greeted a sergeant without using the proper title, and because of that, the instructor yelled, "Start pushing!"

Push-ups until they said stop.

My clothes, my face, my hair — drenched like I had just climbed out of a swimming pool.

It was a full day of conditioning — seeing who they could train mentally and who they could break emotionally. At that point, we knew they were the enemies, and we were all we had.

Days went by. Numbers dropped.

Guys with military backgrounds quit.

Strong men quit.

Loud men quit.

As the numbers got smaller, the class got harder.

After four weeks, we were down to sixteen people. I tried to befriend the only other woman because being surrounded by men was intimidating. One day I called her because I was having a hard time. We vented. She felt the same way. But the next day she never showed up. I called her over and over trying to talk her into staying, but she stopped answering. I was pissed. That's when I realized — it was everybody for themselves.

When she didn't show, the instructors pulled me aside. It was the first time they talked to me like a human being. They wanted me to talk her out of quitting before she lost her job. But I had already tried. And at that point, all my energy had to go toward pushing myself through.

One of the strongest female sergeants at the academy pulled me to the side and told me "You're not quitting."

When the guys realized I was the only woman left, they took me under their wings. They made sure I didn't fail or give up. I became the princess of the academy. They were faster and stronger, but anytime I fell behind, some of them slowed down so I could catch up. I got more love there than I was getting at home.

A month in, we started Defensive Tactics. Being the only woman meant I had to go hands-on with a man. That's when I met Edward. He became my accountability partner. He practiced with me so this other guy — the one who made me uncomfortable — couldn't. Edward pushed me, supported me, and made me feel safe.

One day during takedowns, Edward took me down wrong. I heard a loud pop.

"Edward, you just broke my ankle!"

He denied it, but I knew.

My ankle swelled up like an elephant. We both knew it was broken, but we didn't want to tell anyone because I knew they'd make me start over in the next academy. I refused.

But the more I limped, the more they noticed.

"Princess! What's wrong with you?" a sergeant yelled down the hallway.

"Ma'am, I hurt my ankle in DT ma'am, but I'm okay."

She told me to show her my ankle.

"Who were you working with?"

"Edward."

Two seconds later she screamed,

"EDWARD! Take Princess to the clinic NOW!"

The doctor confirmed it — broken.

I cried immediately.

"I can't start over. I can't quit."

Edward apologized over and over.

I went back to the academy in a walking boot.

My sergeant shook her head.

I kept repeating, "Ma'am, I can't start over."

The lieutenant came in.

"Don't beat yourself up. If we have to love on you longer, we will. But you may have to go through the next academy."

"I'm fine. I'm finishing this one."

From that day forward, Edward was responsible for me. We grew close — like best friends. Neither of us was looking for love. He carried my bags every day.

When I went home, Dro asked what happened.

"I hurt myself."

He shook his head.

"I told you this ain't for you."

I put my head down and tended to my kids.

Weeks passed. I adjusted to the academy with my injury. One day Dro didn't come home, so I took the girls to Daddy's house so I wouldn't be late. Dro wasn't working. All I asked was that he keep the girls on my academy days.

I called him over and over. He was somewhere sloppy drunk. I told Daddy reluctantly because I knew he'd be mad.

Daddy took the girls and told me to stay the night to rest and focus. I declined. I was tired.

I went home and slept. Around 3:30 a.m., I heard keys. I got up, played my gospel music, and started getting ready. I didn't say a word to Dro — not out of anger, but exhaustion. His behavior had become normal.

"You don't wanna talk about this?" he asked.

"No, not really."

He kept trying to talk. I ignored him, trying not to let anything ruin my day.

Then he started yelling in my face, backing me into a corner. I broke away, grabbed my bag, and headed for the door. He started throwing things — whatever he could grab.

I walked outside. Backpack on.

He pushed me down the stairs — even with my broken ankle.

I got up and kept going.

He yanked on my car door.

I reversed.

He climbed on the hood.

I drove 10–15 mph.

He flew off.

I looked in the rearview mirror — he was lying in the street.

For a split second, I thought he was dead.

I stopped.

Got out.

He jumped up and started pushing me again.

I pushed him back.

He got in my car and drove it into the driveway.

But my keys were in my pocket.

I limped back, got in, and pulled off — leaving him standing in the doorway looking stupid.

I called Edward.

Crying.

Yelling.

Shaking.

He was the only one who could calm me down.

I was mentally and emotionally gone.

The lessons life gave me for free:

1.   Silence is louder than a speech

2.   Protect your peace

3.   When people show you who they really are... believe them

---

2 Corinthians 12:9-10

"But he said to me, "My grace is sufficient for you, for my power is made perfect in weakness." Therefore I will boast all the more gladly about my weaknesses, so that Christ's power may rest on me. That is why, for Christ's sake, I delight in weaknesses, in insults, in hardships, in persecutions, in difficulties. For when I am weak, then I am strong."

CHAPTER 9

"HE MET ME WHILE I WAS BECOMING"

After the chaos with Dro that morning, I went back home after the academy exhausted — mentally, emotionally, spiritually. Daddy met me there to drop off the girls. He hugged them, hugged me, and left. I didn't know that the next few minutes would change everything.

When I walked inside, six hood dudes were standing around while Dro cut hair in the kitchen like it was a barbershop. The energy was thick, uncomfortable, and loud. Dro was still mad about the altercation earlier, stomping around the house, slamming things, making sure I knew he was upset. I didn't feed into it. I didn't argue. I didn't match his energy.

I just said, "You doing a lot."

That one sentence set him off.

He started yelling, "Get the fuck out!" over and over, raging through the house.

He was putting me out of my own home.

But instead of fear, I felt relief.

Real relief.

Because I didn't have to figure out how to leave — he had just opened the door for me.

I called Daddy immediately.

"I'm ready. I'm packing me and the girls' stuff now. Come get us."

Daddy must've flown there. It felt like he had been parked across the street waiting for the call. He stormed in, and I only had time to grab two bags — a few clothes for me and the girls. I told him I needed more, and he said,

"What's nice comes twice. Leave all that stuff here."

And just like that, I walked away from the life that had been draining me for years.

I had to get comfortable with being uncomfortable, living in Daddy and Gina's basement for the rest of the academy. It wasn't glamorous. It wasn't easy. But it was safe. And at that point in my life, safety was priceless.

I disappeared from my whole family except Morris.

Everyone else was against me.

Everyone else blamed me for Mama and Daddy's divorce.

Everyone else had something to say about my choices, my life, my pain.

And while I was rebuilding myself, Dro and Mama got closer — talking about me behind my back, bonding over their bitterness, Mama discussing Daddy and Gina with him like he was her confidant. It hurt, but I had to keep going.

I was still waking up.

Still showing up.

Still pushing through the academy with a broken ankle, a broken heart, and a broken home.

And despite every obstacle, Edward made sure of it.

He started paying for hotel rooms so I wouldn't have to make that hour drive back and forth. He helped me study. He pushed me physically. He comforted me mentally and emotionally. He didn't judge me. He didn't question me. He didn't make me feel like a burden.

He just showed up — consistently, quietly, intentionally.

And once he came around, I started passing tests with ease.

Not because it got easier, but because I finally had someone who believed in me without conditions. Someone who saw me — the real me — not the broken version, not the tired version, not the version trying to hold everything together.

He saw the woman I was becoming.

And in that moment, I knew I loved Edward.

Not in a rushed way.

Not in a rebound way.

Not in a way that needed to be defined.

But in a way that felt safe.

In a way that felt earned.

In a way that felt like peace.

He was my calm in the storm.

The first person in a long time who didn't add to my chaos — he helped me rise above it.

He met me while I was becoming.

And he didn't flinch at the process.

Towards the end of the academy, me and Edward had been through it all — the struggling times, the good ones, the long nights, the early mornings, the pressure, the pain, the growth. We had become each other's anchor without even trying.

When it came time for us to be maced, it was the worst day for both of us. The burn, the blindness, the panic — it was like our bodies were on fire. All we could do was call out for each other, blind and spitting excessively, trying to breathe through the pain.

All I heard was,

"Babe, where you at? Feel my hand."

And in that moment — through the fire, the tears, the chaos — I knew Edward fell in love too.

He was my person.

And I was his.

Which made walking across that stage with him even more special. The support. The love. The encouragement. It was beyond anything I had ever experienced. The only other man who ever went that hard for me was Daddy.

Daddy was able to pin me — both of us crying, hugging each other tighter than we ever had. And Edward graduated the police academy right beside me.

Standing side by side, we stepped into our future together.

DPD welcomed us with love and open arms.

— ◆ —

Ruth 2:12
"May the Lord repay you for what you have done. May you be richly rewarded by the Lord, the God of Israel, under whose wings you have come to take refuge."

CHAPTER 10

"WHEN STRENGTH LEARNED MY NAME"

Peace didn't come by accident.

It came through obedience, faith, and endurance—through choosing to keep going when God could have allowed me to stop.

Completing my second police academy was more than a milestone; it was a confirmation. God was not just preparing me for a badge—He was preparing me for responsibility, leadership, and purpose. Every drill, every test, every exhausting moment refined my discipline and strengthened my character. This time, I didn't walk across that stage trying to prove I belonged. I knew I did. God had already gone before me and made the path certain.

My career no longer felt like survival—it felt like calling.

I learned that strength doesn't mean hardness. It means consistency. It means integrity when no one is watching. It means serving with humility and courage. The academy didn't just shape me into an officer—it helped me step fully into the woman God designed me to be: confident, capable, and steady in her purpose.

And in the middle of this alignment, God sent me love.

Not a love that competed with my ambition, but one that honored it. My soulmate didn't ask me to shrink, slow down, or choose between him and my calling. He prayed for me, supported me, and stood proud beside me. Our love grew in discipline, respect, and shared faith. It felt safe to dream with him. It felt natural to build with him.

For the first time, love felt like partnership—not pressure.

God showed me that when love is ordained, it strengthens your purpose instead of distracting you from it. With him, I was able to be both strong and soft, focused and fulfilled. I didn't lose myself in love—I found deeper clarity.

I am grateful for those God placed around me—the ones who encouraged me through long days, prayed over my future, believed in my ability, and reminded me why I started. Their support was God's hand extended through people, carrying me when my strength ran low.

This chapter is about alignment.

Alignment between faith and career.

Alignment between love and purpose.

Alignment between who I prayed to become and who I now am.

I found peace when I trusted God's timing. I found confidence when I accepted His calling. I found love when I allowed God to choose with me, not for me. And I found rest in knowing that nothing I endured was wasted.

Now I move forward—grounded in faith, fulfilled in love, and committed to a career of service. I walk into my future covered by God, supported by love, and guided by purpose.

This is not the end of my story.

This is the beginning of the life God promised—

one built on faith, love, and calling.

Deuteronomy 31:8

"The Lord himself goes before you and will be with you; he will never leave you nor forsake you. Do not be afraid; do not be discouraged."

ACKNOWLEDGEMENTS

To My Daddy,

Thank you for being my foundation, my protector, and my steady place in a world that hasn't always been gentle. Your love shaped who I am, your lessons carried me through moments I didn't think I'd survive, and your strength gave me something to lean on when mine felt gone. Even when words were few, your presence spoke loudly. Everything I am becoming holds pieces of you, and I carry your love with me in every step of this journey. This book is written with gratitude, love, and honor for you—always.

To My Mama,

Thank you for standing by me even when our hearts clashed and words failed. Though we've had our struggles, your love has been a quiet force shaping me, teaching me resilience, forgiveness, and the depth of connection that comes from enduring the hard moments together. Even in the times when we were distant or hurt each other, I want to honor my mother. Your love, though sometimes complicated, has been my anchor.

Thank you for showing me strength, for your patience, and for being a part of my story—even in the chapters that were painful.

To My Brother,

Thank you for being my safe place when the world felt heavy and my strength when I felt like I had none left. You saw me in moments I tried to hide, believed in me when I was unsure of myself, and never let me forget who I am. Your love, protection, and quiet sacrifices carried me through more than you'll ever know. This journey holds pieces of your heart in it, and I am forever grateful to walk this life knowing I have you beside me.

To My Soulmate,

Thank you for loving me with a depth that felt both fierce and gentle, for choosing me even when things were heavy, and for standing ten toes down when it mattered most. Your presence steadied my heart, your love softened my scars, and your belief in me lit fires in places I had gone quiet. You didn't just walk beside me—you held me, protected me, and reminded me what it feels like to be truly seen and chosen. This book carries pieces of our love, our lessons, and our growth. I am grateful for you in ways words will never fully capture.

To My Children,

You are my heart, my light, and my reason for everything I do. Every step I take, every challenge I face, and every dream I chase is because of you. Your laughter, love, and belief in me—

even without knowing it—push me to rise higher and be the best version of myself. You inspire me to keep going, to hold on to my purpose, and to show you what strength, dedication, and love look like. This journey is for you, and I carry you in every page, every word, and every success.

To My TAC Staff and Police Instructors,

I extend my sincere gratitude for your leadership, discipline, and unwavering commitment to excellence. You pushed me when I was tired, corrected me when it mattered most, and held me to standards that demanded growth. Through structure, accountability, and pressure, you sharpened my skills, strengthened my mindset, and built the mental toughness required for this profession. You saw potential in me even when I questioned myself, and every challenge, lesson, and expectation helped shape my confidence, resilience, and sense of duty. The foundation you provided will continue to guide me throughout my career. I carry your lessons forward with pride, respect, and gratitude as I step into what's next.

To My Co Writer

My sister, Sheley Hollins-Boyd, also known as the Author Reina Nativa —thank you for believing in this story as deeply as I did. Thank you for your patience, your honesty, and the countless moments you showed up when the words felt heavy. This work is stronger because of your voice, your perspective, and your willingness to walk this journey with me. Collaboration isn't just shared writing—it's shared trust, shared vision, and shared growth. I'm grateful for your commitment, your creativity, and the way you helped bring this story to life. This book carries both of our hearts, and I wouldn't have wanted to create it with anyone else

DISCLAIMER

This book is a personal memoir. It reflects the author's memories, interpretations, and experiences during the periods described. While every effort has been made to portray events and individuals accurately, some names, identifying details, timelines, and locations have been changed or combined to protect privacy. Any resemblance to actual persons, living or dead, is coincidental and unintentional.

The author does not claim to provide legal, medical, psychological, or professional advice. The content of this book is for storytelling purposes only and should not be used as a substitute for professional guidance. The author and publisher assume no responsibility for any actions taken by readers based on the material presented.

The events, conversations, and emotions described are true to the author's recollection; however, memory is imperfect. Certain scenes have been reconstructed, condensed, or dramatized for clarity and narrative flow. The author's perspective is her own and does not represent the views of any agency, employer, department, or organization mentioned.

No part of this book is intended to harm, defame, or misrepresent any individual or institution. The author's intention is solely to share her personal journey, growth, and lived experiences. Readers acknowledge that they engage with this material at their own discretion.